IN THE GARDEN

by Latoya Green
illustrated by Andrea Wesson

Orlando   Boston   Dallas   Chicago   San Diego

Visit *The Learning Site!*
www.harcourtschool.com

It's spring! Let's grow a vegetable garden! You can plant different vegetables in the ground. When they're ripe, you can eat them. How does your garden grow? Let's find out.

Find a good spot for your garden. The ground must have a lot of soil. It cannot have a lot of rocks or sand. It must get a lot of sunlight, too. This spot looks fine!

Now you can prepare the soil. First, pull up the grass and weeds that grow in the ground. Then, dig up the soil with a shovel. Dig about 12 inches deep into the ground.

Next, break up the soil into tiny
pieces. Then, rake the soil to make it
smooth and fine. Fine soil will grow
fine vegetables!

Now you are ready to plant. What will you grow in your garden? Choose the vegetables you like to eat. Do you like spaghetti sauce? You can grow tomatoes! What about salad? Plant lettuce, cucumbers, and carrots.

Many vegetables grow from seeds.
Plant the seeds in rows. Make holes in
the soil with your fingers. Push a seed
into each hole. Then cover it with soil.
Mark each row so you know what kind
of vegetable will be growing there.

Now you must water your seeds. Your vegetables will not grow without water. Some vegetable seeds need more water than others do. Find out how much water to give each kind of seed.

The best time to water is in the morning or early afternoon. Then the sun can dry the water on the soil. Do not water after the sun sets. Then the soil will stay too wet all night!

How is your garden growing? It
seems to be growing well! The seeds
have sprouted. Many of the vegetable
plants are coming up from the
ground. You can see small green
leaves growing on each plant.

The plants have grown taller. The leaves are much bigger than before. Did you notice that there are flowers growing on many of the plants? In a few weeks, you will see tiny vegetables. Soon the vegetables will grow big enough to eat!

Some plants have grown better than others. This tomato plant got the right amount of water and sunlight. Its leaves look fresh and green. Why do you think they look that way?

This carrot plant got very little water and sunlight. Its leaves look dry and dark. Why do you think they look that way? What do you think you will find when you dig up this carrot?

It's the end of summer! How has
your garden grown? It has grown very
well. Most vegetables grow above the
ground. You can see that these
vegetables are ripe. It's time to pick
them off the plants.

Other vegetables grow below the ground. How can you tell when they are ripe? Look at the plant leaves. When the leaves are dried out, it's time to pull up or dig up these vegetables.

What's the best part of growing a vegetable garden? As soon as you wash off the dirt, the vegetables are ready to eat! You don't even have to cook them. You can make a fresh salad. Put in beans, beets, and carrots. Add lettuce, tomatoes, and onions. Enjoy your delicious garden!